Unconditional Surrender

Mark and Kathy,

Thank you for
your devotion to the
Saints Prison Ministry.

Love and Hugs

June

Unconditional Surrender

Dale M. Glading

Word Association Publishers
www.wordassociation.com

ISBN: 978-1-59571-190-8
Library of Congress Control Number: 2007925482

Word Association Publishers
205 5th Avenue
Tarentum, PA 15084
www.wordassociation.com

Dedication

To my wife Deanna, who has embraced God's call on my life as her own. Her years of sacrifice for our family and The Saints Prison Ministry will be richly rewarded in Glory.

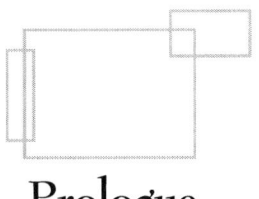

Prologue

"To present the Gospel of Jesus Christ to prisoners through athletics and to provide them with opportunities for spiritual growth." This mission statement has served The Saints Prison Ministry well for the past two decades. However, before reading about the 20-year history of our organization, I believe that it's important for you to understand the rationale behind our mission statement.

Surveys show that 80% of America's 2.4 million prisoners refuse to attend a conventional religious program such as a chapel service or a Bible study. Admittedly, these programs are sorely needed, but they are better designed for discipling believers than for evangelizing unbelievers.

So, what about the other 1.9 million inmates? If they aren't in the prison chapel, where are they and how can we best reach them for Jesus Christ? Based on 20 years of prison ministry experience, I can categorically say that many of them can be found in the prison gym or weather permitting, in the recreation yard. And since the average inmate in the United States today is a male in his early 20's, chances are he is playing some type of sport in his free time.

What better way to reach these men with the gospel than to compete with them on the athletic field, earning their respect while showing that we are genuinely interested in them as individuals? This simple formula has allowed our sports teams to witness to over 200,000 prisoners across the United States and Canada, with more than 15,000 of them making professions of faith in Jesus Christ. As a result, men who would never darken the door of the prison chapel are now hearing and responding to God's Word.

Since our inception in 1987, we have also followed a basic creed: you cannot lead a man to Christ without seeking to disciple him. In fact, it is both our responsibility and our privilege to do so. That's why we have operated our own Bible Correspondence School for the past 20 years. Currently, an estimated 2,500 prisoners are studying God's Word with us in either English or Spanish and our inmate mailing list has grown to over 25,000.

Nationally, seven out of every 10 prisoners are rearrested within four years of their release. This number drops dramatically to 35 – 40% for those inmates who make a genuine profession of faith in Jesus Christ while incarcerated. For those fortunate enough to be welcomed and mentored by a Bible-believing church post-release, the recidivism rate falls even farther to 10 – 15%.

To me, that is a strong argument for a creative and comprehensive prison ministry that meets men and women where they are, not where we want them to be. Following Paul's admonition in I Corinthians 9:22, The Saints Prison Ministry seeks to be "all things to all men, that we might by all means save some." (NKJV)

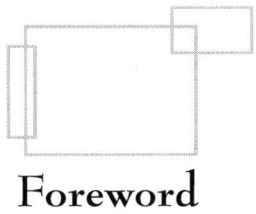

Foreword

In 2002, a cultural phenomenon within Christian churches worldwide started with the release of Pastor Rick Warren's *"A Purpose Driven Life"*. Millions of individuals, and thousands of churches have since used this devotional study to wrestle with the meaning and implications of what is contained succinctly in the very first sentence of that book:

"It's not about you."

From the moment we are born, we become the center of our own physical universe and are encouraged to succeed – to 'look out for #1'. In this one statement, a lifetime of lessons in self-esteem and pride are challenged like a cold cup of water thrown into our faces. Indeed, our cultural and personal priorities have grown far out of alignment with God's design for our lives; we have sacrificed the relationship He desires to have with us on the altars of convenience, expedience and earthly success. Such a wake-up call is desperately needed amongst those who claim to follow Christ.

So, what *does* it look like when we begin to yield our own goals and desires in order to place God on His throne in our everyday lives? The book that you are now holding is the story of one man's experience as he comes face-to-face with the truth of this statement – and of the unlikely miracles that lay in store for those who submit their will and pride to a

God who truly loves you and wants His Best for you. As you will see in Dale's account, when we respond to God's call to surrender – *unconditionally* – we are not rewarded with a life free from trials and setbacks. We are, however, guaranteed that God will not abandon the heart that follows His call – even though there are times when we may not always see Him there...

I can tell you from my own experience that this unlikely ministry is like a breath of fresh air for today's church. Assembling ordinary men – painters, plumbers, schoolteachers, computer jockeys, professionals, supervisors, laborers, and more – and taking them behind the razor wire and turreted walls of our nation's prisons to spread God's love through a simple game and a willingness to speak boldly for Jesus Christ; this is as close a parallel to the early church as I have ever seen in today's society. It is a bold move. There are a thousand reasons to think it wouldn't work. But it does.

I have personally witnessed hardened men weeping in front of their cellmates as the awesome love of Christ penetrates their heart's defenses – and I've embraced them in prayer as they genuinely accepted His grace and forgiveness. I have likewise seen those who – like me – have similarly answered that unlikely Call to rise up from our sofas and office desks, leave our families and comfort zones, and willingly go to places where society tells us we should dedicate our lives to staying away from. I have seen myself – and men like me – grow from passive bystanders in our grand church buildings into bold preachers, better fathers, more faithful husbands...

We did not start this ministry, but we are grateful that through Dale's unconditional surrender God has blessed his efforts for the past 20 years. I was not there at the beginning, but have been privileged to come alongside as a helper and co-laborer in this mission. I pray as Dale's story unfolds before you, that you, too will be challenged to take that step of faith... to see what unlikely blessings the Lord has in store for you.

Who am I? It doesn't matter. I am just one more follower who has been touched and blessed to be associated with Dale and the Saints Prison Ministry – and through that I've learned that 'it's not about me', either...

A friend, a teammate, a follower of Jesus Christ

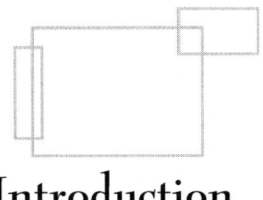

Introduction

Growing up, I had no illusions of becoming a Major League baseball player. Despite hundreds of hours of backyard wiffleball and sandlot games, it occurred to me at a very early age that I simply wasn't good enough. In fact, I didn't even play Little League until I was 11. Thanks to Sam Hamill's coaching, I hit a robust .333 for the Cardinals that season and learned to rock when I pitched like Robin Roberts.

The following year I made the traveling All-Star team, the Bankers, and batted somewhere around .065 (no, that's not a misprint.) However, because I pitched our 2-18 team to one of our two wins that season, I was named our Most Valuable Player. Or maybe it was because my dad always bought gas at Lou Chaplick's service station. Lou was our coach.

Sports, and baseball in particular, continued to fascinate me throughout my childhood years. So did American history. I especially enjoyed reading the biographies of great Americans. Whether I was visiting our local library or buying armloads of paperbacks at a used bookstore in Camden, I devoured stories about athletes and inventors, statesmen and pioneers. My heroes were men like Daniel Boone, Thomas Edison, Lou Gehrig and Robert E. Lee. I could even recite the U.S. presidents in order, perhaps hoping to be one some day.

And so, up until my 16th birthday, my life's course was set or so I thought. I would go to college, major in political science, get a law degree and then run for political office. However, all that changed as a result of a simple conversation I had that summer with my favorite uncle.

My Uncle Wayne was my favorite uncle for one simple reason – he loved baseball. In fact, he was the only person I knew who could recite more sports trivia than I could. When he was in town, Uncle Wayne would often stop by our house and we would talk baseball by the hour. Occasionally, he would pull a glove out of his trunk and allow me to pitch to him. Just like my dad, he always gave me the borderline strikes.

During one such visit, Uncle Wayne casually mentioned that several colleges were now offering a new major called "Sports Administration." That quickly, my life's goal changed from wanting to be a career politician to wanting to work in the front office of a professional sports team. Within a matter of months, I had been accepted at St. John's University in Jamaica, New York, fully intending to be the next general manager of the New York Yankees.

What happened over the next 10 years doesn't make sense from a human standpoint. That God would take an ambitious yet self-centered young man and use him to start an athletic prison ministry is a testament to His mercy and grace. Indeed, what He has accomplished during the first 20 years of The Saints Prison Ministry is nothing short of miraculous.

My reason for writing this book is two-fold. First, I want to glorify God by recalling how He raised up and continues to bless the Saints ministry. Second, I want to encourage others to step out in faith and answer God's call on their lives. Simply put, if He can use an imperfect vessel like me, imagine what He can do in and through YOU!

In order to accurately tell the story of The Saints Prison Ministry, it is necessary for me to tell my own story first. By no means is this book meant to be self-promoting. Rather, it will become readily apparent to even the most casual reader that any successes The Saints have experienced over the years are due solely to God, and any failures can be attributed almost exclusively to me.

Perhaps I Corinthians 1:27 says it best. "But God has chosen the foolish things of the world to put to shame the wise, and God has chosen the weak things of the world to put to shame the things which are mighty." (NKJV)

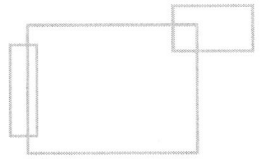

Conception and Birth
September 1986 – June 1987

"And you will seek Me and find Me, when you search for Me with all your heart." Jeremiah 29:13 (NKJV)

January 1862. Brigadier General Ulysses Grant and Flag Officer Andrew Foote are appointed to jointly lead a force of more than 15,000 foot soldiers and seven gunboats. Their mission is to capture Forts Henry and Donelson, which guard the Tennessee and Cumberland rivers. The commander of the Confederate garrison, Brigadier General Lloyd Tilghman, soon realizes that his plight is hopeless. And so, under a flag of truce, he requests the terms for surrender.

Because General Grant and his men are bogged down in the mud, still miles away from Fort Henry, it is left to Officer Foote to negotiate the surrender terms. However, he refuses to do so. Instead, he sends back a terse, one-sentence reply. "No sir, your surrender will be unconditional!"

It was our first vacation as a married couple and for reasons long since forgotten, we decided on Williamsburg, Virginia as our destination. Since we were newlyweds, it didn't matter to us that our two-man pup tent was really designed for 1 1/2 people. Our days were filled with sightseeing for me and shopping for Deanna. Evenings were spent swimming in the icy-cold pool and doing crossword puzzles by lantern light. We also passed time strolling hand in hand through the campground, dreaming of the day when we would own a trailer of our own.

Following one such walk, my spirit became restless, so much so that I mentioned it to Deanna. I didn't go into detail, because I wasn't sure of the details myself. I simply told her that, "I need to be alone with the Lord." And so, I climbed a small dirt road on the outskirts of the campground and started to speak out loud to God.

"Father," I said, "all I want is what You want. Please take my life and do whatever you want with it."

I returned from this "mountaintop" experience unchanged and yet, changed for all eternity. By simply emptying myself of my own plans and ambitions, I had opened the door for God to accomplish far more with my life than I could have ever dreamed or imagined.

Years later, The Saints Basketball Team was en route home from one of our Florida crusades. I was seated on the plane next to Todd Tangert, who was our board president at the time.

"Why do you think God chose you to start the Saints," Todd asked matter-of-factly. My thoughts immediately returned to September 1986 and that dirt road in Williamsburg. "All I can think of is that I was willing," I answered.

Almost nine months to the day following that camping trip to Williamsburg, The Saints Prison Ministry was born. So was our first child, Bethany Nicole Glading. I blame the pup tent.

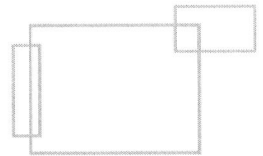

The Brady Bunch Years
September 1959 – February 1977

"Before I formed you in the womb I knew you; before you were born I sanctified you." Jeremiah 1:5 (NKJV)

Ozzie and Harriett had long since ended their successful run as the prototypical American family and the dysfunctional Simpsons had yet to appear on our television screens. No, if there was one TV family that we could identify with it was The Brady Bunch.

A father, a mother and six kids, three of each gender. We didn't have a dog and we certainly couldn't afford a housekeeper named Alice, but the similarities remained. As the fifth child and the youngest boy, I was Bobby Brady.

At the risk of idealizing my childhood, I honestly wouldn't change much about my growing-up years. Merchantville, New Jersey was a great place to be a kid and despite being surrounded by such larger towns as Cherry Hill and Pennsauken, we felt insulated from the outside world.

There was never a question that our parents loved us. Sure, we had our share of difficulties, some of them dealing with my younger sister's battle with epilepsy. And, looking back, I'm sure there were financial struggles as my dad tried to support a family of eight on a single income. But we were happy and most things seemed to come relatively easy for the Glading family.

My dad was William Alfred Glading. An only child, he was named for his father, William John, who was named for his dad, William Henry Harrison. Imagine my grandmother's disappointment when my father named his three sons, Scott, Gary and Dale!

Growing up during the Depression hadn't soured my dad's optimism, but serving three years in the South Pacific during World War II had hardened him a bit as had the pressures of raising a large family. It would take a born-again experience when he was in his early fifties to finally soften some of those hard edges. I still admire my dad for acknowledging his need for Christ at such an age and especially for the way he "made up for lost time" during the last 25 years of his life.

Like so many other servicemen returning from the war, my dad landed a job, got married and started a family. Noreen came first, followed by Scott, Gary and Cheryl in rapid succession. Exactly 365 days later, I came along. To this day, Cheryl still refers to me as her "first birthday present!" Finally, Diane was born, completing our family in 1960.

The "Glading Tribe", as my dad nicknamed us, grew up in a series of houses. However, most of my childhood was spent at 107 St. James Avenue in Merchantville. A large Dutch colonial situated on a tree-lined street, it gave my siblings and me a real sense of security. I think I could still walk through that old house blindfolded without bumping into a single wall.

Regardless of where we lived, my mother made sure that it wasn't just a house; it was a home. June MacDowell grew up in Camden, New Jersey, the daughter of a fireman and his wife. Perhaps because her own childhood was so unhappy, she was determined to make things better for her kids. She and my dad met on a blind date, arranged by his father, and they made a great team. I guess you could say that her open affection perfectly balanced his tough love.

Outside our home, several factors helped shape the lives of my brothers, my sisters and me. First, and to a lesser extent, was the church we attended. We were regular attendees, but I can't ever remember looking forward to going. In hindsight, I guess it was because the services were full of ritual and devoid of relationship.

The other dominant influence on our lives was school. Merchantville was so small that eventually the high school was forced to close due to declining enrollment. However, that didn't stop Noreen from excelling on the athletic field or Scott from starring in the school plays. Gary did the best of all, being named class valedictorian at neighboring Pennsauken High School.

While I fell short of Gary's academic record and never played varsity sports, school was still where I excelled and my Type-A personality was formed. I earned good grades and learned early on how to win a teacher's approval. This pattern of hard work reaping academic success continued throughout my school years. In fact, I was named Most Likely to Succeed at both my 9th and 12th grade graduations. From there it was off to college where I earned a Bachelor's degree in Community Recreation from Temple University in 1981.

However, something dramatic happened just three months before I graduated from high school. I met Jesus Christ.

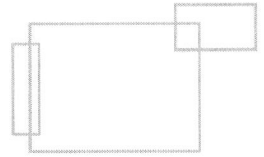

Now I Can Use You
March 1977 – March 1982

"The fear of the Lord is the instruction of wisdom, and before honor is humility." Proverbs 15:33 (NKJV)

It was March 1977, a Sunday as I recall, and I hurried home from church with one thought in mind. Changing quickly out of my dress clothes, I was about to head out to the local park to scrounge up a ball game when my mother stopped me cold in my tracks.

"Your brother Gary would like to hold a family Bible study," she said in a tone of voice that told me that there was no room for negotiation. And so, we gathered around our dining room table and listened as my brother started to preach.

Actually, he didn't preach, it was more like an explanation. Step by step, so nervous that his voice quivered with each word, Gary laid out for us God's plan of salvation. Between glances at the clock, I followed along in my head, trusting that what he was reading from the Bible was accurate. After all, I didn't have a Bible of my own or if I did, I sure didn't know where to find it.

I had noticed a recent change in Gary, things like him wearing a large cross on the outside of his clothes. He had even started carrying a Bible to school with him (maybe that's where mine went?) In any case, he apparently wanted the rest of us to experience what he had.

After a period of time, we were dismissed from the table. But instead of heading outside to play, I climbed the stairs to my room. If what my brother had said was true, then playing ball could wait. And so, there at the foot of my bed in front of a large picture of Jesus, I accepted Christ as my Savior.

I wish I could say that my life changed from that moment on. Certainly, my spiritual condition did, as did my eternal destiny (yes, I believe in eternal security!) However, I probably sinned more in the next five years than in my first 17 years on this planet. Yet, God had begun a "good work" in me (Philippians 1:6) and He would slowly but surely gain control of my life. First, however, He had to deal with my pride or more specifically, to break me of it.

As I mentioned earlier, I had enrolled at St. John's University in New York City in September 1977. Coming from the warmth and security of a large family, St. John's was a rude awakening for me. No longer was I living in a three-story house in quaint Merchantville, New Jersey. Instead, I was living in a basement apartment in Queens, New York, in the same neighborhood where David Berkowitz, the infamous Son of Sam, had recently murdered a number of co-eds. Ironically, we would later encounter David at Sullivan Correctional Facility in Fallsburg, New York when he attended one of our softball games. During the intervening years, he had become a born-again Christian and was even enrolled in our Bible Correspondence School for a time.

I continued to earn good grades at St. John's, but the Big

Apple - or any big city for that matter - simply wasn't for me. And so, I was soon abandoning this commuter school for the familiarity of our South Jersey home every weekend. After two years, driven by both homesickness and my first serious romance, I transferred to Temple University in Philadelphia.

Around this time, I began attending my first real Bible-believing church at the invitation of my sister's boyfriend. Cheryl had recently committed her life to Christ as had my dad and my sister Diane. It was like a domino effect as one Glading after another trusted Him as Savior. Before long, most of us were regulars at St. Paul's Evangelical Bible Church and I even joined their softball team.

However, despite becoming a member at St. Paul's, I was still living "in the world" so to speak. Sure, I had coaxed my girlfriend into making a profession of faith, but there wasn't much difference between the unsaved Dale Glading and the born-again version. It soon became apparent that God was going to have to do something radical in order to get my attention.

Two weeks before Easter 1981, I accompanied my father to a local jewelry store to pick out an engagement ring. Commensurate with my station in life as an unemployed college senior, the ring boasted a 1/4 carat diamond. It was my intention to present it to my girlfriend on Easter Sunday inside a porcelain Easter egg I had already purchased.

It was as if God was running out of time. If He didn't act quickly, no matter how painful it would be, my life would soon be heading down the wrong path, perhaps irrevocably.

Still, nothing could have prepared me for the phone call I was to receive just days later. It was from my girlfriend, and she wanted to break up.

The next few weeks were a blur as I tried to get ready for final exams while feeling as if my heart had been ripped from my chest. Somehow, I managed to graduate with high honors, but I was so devastated that I didn't even attend the graduation ceremonies.

Months passed as I tried to focus on landing a job, but to no avail. It was as if I had said to the world, "Here I am" and the world had replied, "Who cares?"

For the next 10 months, I worked a series of part-time jobs, everything from driving a floral delivery van to making change at an arcade in the mall. It was degrading work for someone who had just graduated Summa Cum Laude from college. And yet, God was doing something wonderful in my life. He was breaking my spirit and ridding me of my pride.

I was as low as I'd ever been in my life to that point. I had no sense of direction and even worse, no one to share my life with.

"Now I can use you," God seemed to say.

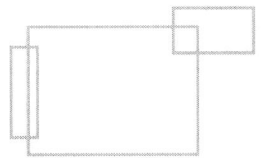

What Do You *Really* Want To Do With Your Life?

April 1982 – January 1983

"Commit your works to the Lord, and your thoughts will be established." Proverbs 16:3 (NKJV)

I was stuck between a rock and a hard place. I had finally landed a full-time job in the recreation and leisure field, specifically as a travel agent with Liberty Travel. However, I wasn't scheduled to start working for several weeks and wouldn't receive a paycheck until I had completed a series of training classes in North Jersey. That meant that I wouldn't have enough money to go with my best friend to Florida for Spring Break.

Now, don't get me wrong. I'm not talking about your typical Spring Break vacation. I'm talking about spending a week or so in Delray Beach with my friend's grandmother and another few days in the Florida Keys with some of his friends from the University of Delaware. Did I mention that his friends were members of InterVarsity Christian Fellowship?

To this day, I don't know why my parents did what they did. All I know is that I will be eternally grateful and that my life was changed as a result.

Figuring that I wouldn't get another vacation until I had completed a full year at the travel agency, my parents loaned me some money and encouraged me to go. And so, I piled into my buddy's car and off we went, two guys and two girls for two weeks in sunny Florida.

Once again, it's not what you're thinking. The girls were sisters in Christ from U of D and the entire two weeks were like a sorely needed retreat. In fact, it was the greatest spiritual high of my life. For on this trip, somewhere between learning the basics of sign language (what else do you do on a 1,000 mile car ride?) and being lost at sea on a catamaran (that's a whole another story), I fell in love with Jesus Christ.

I returned home on Easter Sunday, just in time to shower and change for church. Despite spending the last 20 hours cramped in a car, there was no way that I was going to miss worshipping my Risen Lord on His Resurrection Day!

That evening I went over to my girlfriend's house – yes, we had reconciled six months earlier – and gave her a loving but firm ultimatum. "We can either start our relationship over with Jesus Christ at the center or we can break up," I said. "Either way is all right with me."

Only by the grace of God could I have uttered those words to a girl who, at one time, had been the absolute center of my universe. However, I now had a new foundation, a Solid Rock (Matthew 7:24-25), upon which my life was built. And so, when she called a few days later to say that she had "outgrown" me, I was able to wish her well and mean it.

Over the next several months, I attended InterVarsity's Friday night "gatherings" in Delaware as often as possible. I was growing spiritually by leaps and bounds, and God even used me to lead a co-worker to Christ at the travel agency.

One day, a friend asked me the following question: "What do you want to do with your life?" Without hesitation I replied, "I'd like to recruit a bunch of Christian softball players, put them on a bus and barnstorm around the country, telling people about Jesus."

My friend looked at me as if to say, "What do you *really* want to do with your life?" In hindsight, I guess I did sound a bit naïve. And yet, little did I know that God was about to grant me the absolute desires of my heart. (Psalm 37:4)

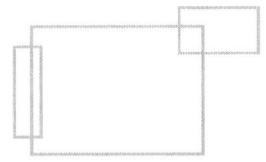

The Back Side of the Desert
February 1983 – May 1987

*"But Moses fled from the face of Pharoah and dwelt in the
land of Midian." Exodus 2:15 (NKJV)*

The Wiley Mission was an outgrowth of the Wiley
Methodist Church, pastored by Rev. John Hackett.
Camden, New Jersey had been hit particularly hard by the
Great Depression and so, Rev. Hackett and his wife decided
to start a soup kitchen to feed the hungry. This fledgling
ministry took on a life of its own and the Hacketts were
soon using an old post office building to accommodate
those needing their help. The Wiley Mission was
incorporated in 1939, and a few years later, the Hacketts
moved the ministry to Marlton, New Jersey where they
opened a home for the aged.

With Rev. Hackett's passing, the mantle of leadership fell
upon his son-in-law, Cecil Gilmore, Sr. "Dad" Gilmore was
an excellent administrator who didn't care much for the
limelight. As a result, his wife Virginia soon became the
face of this growing ministry. In fact, "Mom" Gilmore did
most of the preaching at the Wiley Church as well as on
their popular radio program.

Eventually, Dad Gilmore retired and was succeeded by his
sons. Cecil, Jr., the eldest, became the church's pastor and
Donald took over the retirement community. Today, a third

son, Douglas, pastors the nondenominational Wiley Church while the youngest son, Gary, serves as Executive Director of the continuing care retirement community. Cecil, Jr., continues to be active as President of Wiley's Board of Trustees.

In November 1982, I had left my position at the travel agency with no other job prospects. I simply knew that a career in the travel industry wasn't for me. Perhaps because he was forced to make a few of my car payments, my father got involved in my job search and soon, I had an interview at the Wiley Christian Retirement Community.

As a personal favor to my dad, Don Gilmore met with me in February 1983. Despite the fact that my degree was not in Therapeutic Recreation, he offered me a position as a part-time Activities Assistant. Needing a job, I accepted it gratefully. However, I started to have second thoughts when I found out that my responsibilities included leading the ladies crafts class! Needless to say, I couldn't have been happier when, just five weeks later, my immediate supervisor took another position within the organization and I was promoted. Not only did that mean that I was now a full-time department head, but I could finally delegate that crafts class to someone else!

Over the next 10 years, my job at Wiley evolved into something that only God could have imagined, let alone orchestrated. Within a few months of being hired from the unemployment line, I was assigned a myriad of other duties including supervising Wiley's volunteer program. I was also tasked with directing the mission's fundraising efforts.

It was in my role as chief fundraiser that I met Bill Sutter, a direct mail consultant. At the time, Bill counted America's Keswick, Philadelphia College of Bible (now Philadelphia Biblical University) and the Atlantic City Rescue Mission among his clients. Today, Bill serves as Executive Director of Friends of Israel, a ministry based in Deptford, New Jersey and dedicated to reaching the Jewish people for Christ and supporting Israel as an independent state.

Don Gilmore had brought Bill in to teach me the fundamentals of direct mail fundraising. He was an excellent mentor and soon, I was writing appeal letters to thousands of Wiley's supporters using Bill's battle-tested techniques.

Around this time, construction began on The Village at Wiley. The culmination of Don Gilmore's dream for Wiley's 55-acre parcel of land, the Village was soon populated with active adults, ages 60 and over. It didn't take much persuasion for Don to allow me to organize overnight trips for these fine folks. And so, in addition to enjoying such vacation spots as Annapolis, Maryland and Hershey, Pennsylvania, I was able to hone the skills I had acquired at the travel agency just a few years earlier. These same skills would later prove helpful in planning our many Saints crusades.

It amazes me to think that I acquired most of the experience I would later need to run an athletic prison ministry by working at a Christian retirement community. But where else could a 23-year old, fresh out of college, have been given the opportunity to manage a small but growing department while overseeing the volunteer and development programs for a multi-million dollar enterprise?

I will be forever grateful to God for my years on the backside of the desert and to the Gilmore family for their unwavering support as I pursued my calling. And that's exactly what it was, a calling.

For around this time, my family had started to attend Haddon Heights Baptist Church where Powers Payton was the Senior Pastor. He was also a fabulous windmill pitcher and I'm glad that I didn't have to face him except during batting practice!

In any case, the church held a missions conference at which Bill Commons was one of the speakers. An administrator with the Association of Baptists for World Evangelism (ABWE), Bill would be the first to tell you that he is not a dynamic orator. However, God spoke through him that night, at least to me. The Holy Spirit was literally leaping within me as Bill gave the altar call. I didn't even wait for the singing to begin, but practically ran down the aisle and dedicated my life to full-time Christian service.

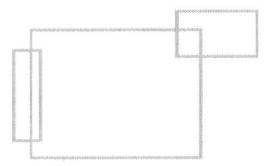

Entering the Race
June 6, 1987

"Therefore we also, since we are surrounded by so great a
cloud of witnesses, let us lay aside every weight, and the
sin which so easily ensnares us, and let us run with
endurance the race that is set before us, looking unto
Jesus, the author and finisher of our faith..."
Hebrews 12:1-2 (NKJV)

During my years at Wiley, the Lord continued to grant me a
vision for starting some type of athletic ministry. I prayed
about it often and would occasionally ask people I respected
for their opinions. Meanwhile, I had met my future
helpmate, Deanna, and after a one-year courtship we were
married on June 29, 1985.

Deanna Truax is the elder of two daughters born to Dean
and Phyllis Truax of Big Cove Tannery, Pennsylvania.
Dean's given name is Floyd, but everybody calls him by his
middle name so as not to confuse him with his father and
namesake.

When I say that Deanna grew up in Big Cove Tannery, what
I mean to say is that's where the nearest post office is
located. To this day, her parents' house is situated on a 15-
acre Christmas tree farm with their closest neighbors being
a quarter mile or so away.

So how did a boy from the Jersey suburbs meet a slender, young girl with auburn hair from farm country? I like to tell people that Deanna was a mail order bride or that our parents had arranged our marriage while we were still kids. But the truth of the matter is that we met at a wedding where I was the best man and she was the pianist. Actually, her grandmother was supposed to play the piano that day, but had backed out because she wasn't used to playing contemporary music. Sometimes I tease Deanna that if the couple being married had selected more traditional hymns, I may have married her grandmother instead!

Our first year of marriage was spent in an apartment in Maple Shade, New Jersey. Then, when Don Gilmore offered us some free staff housing on Wiley's property, we moved to Marlton. It was there, living in a two-bedroom apartment above a maintenance garage, that we welcomed our first two children into the world.

Bethany Nicole Glading was born at 4:10 PM on June 27, 1987 and Matthew Travis Glading followed two years later on August 1, 1989. For the record, had Bethany been a boy she would have been named Daniel. Conversely, Matthew would have been named Kimberly.

Between the time we were married and the time Bethany was born, God continued to burden me with a desire to launch an athletic ministry. I was daydreaming about it by day, and dreaming for real about it by night. Not so coincidentally, the men's softball team at our church was disbanding, leaving a number of young athletes with no place to play. Clearly, God was orchestrating events and moving in my heart at the same time.

Like Moses and Gideon however, I wasn't convinced that I was up to the task. I truly loved the Lord and enjoyed playing sports of all kinds, but just how was I supposed to combine these two great loves?

Around this time, I attended a missions conference at an inner-city church in Philadelphia where a man by the name of John DeNofa was scheduled to present a workshop. John was a member of the Christian Nine, a fast-pitch softball team that played in a local league for the purpose of witnessing to other ballplayers. The Christian Nine also conducted an annual trip to Mexico to play against some club teams there. I spoke to John afterwards and God used him to further excite me about the possibilities.

Another gentleman that God used to confirm my calling was Chuck Gordon. Chuck was in his early 40's at the time, but had just been introduced to the joys of fast-pitch softball. Specifically, Chuck was training to become a windmill pitcher and needed a team to showcase his newfound talent. Another meeting at a local church ensued, this time in Turnersville, New Jersey.

I don't recall if an actual team was formed that night, although I did play an exhibition game shortly thereafter with Chuck and some other Christian softball players. However, I distinctly remember leaving that meeting in Turnersville with a name ringing inside my head. If God ever directed me to form an all-Christian softball team, I told myself, it was sure to be called The South Jersey Saints.

Still, I continued to wait on the Lord, not quite sure what my next step should be. All I knew was that this God-given vision was starting to monopolize my thoughts. In fact, when meeting with a realtor friend of mine around this time, I described my feelings as "eating, sleeping and dreaming" about the idea.

Finally, God used the most elementary thing to get me moving – an editorial cartoon in a newspaper published by WVCH, a Christian radio station in the area. It showed three athletes running a race with captions beside each one. The first two sprinters had fallen by the wayside, both making excuses for their lack of success. However, the third runner exclaimed, "I did it!" as he broke the tape. God spoke to me through that simple cartoon, which eventually found itself posted on our refrigerator door. After five years of praying and seeking godly counsel, it was time to enter the race.

And so, on June 6, 1987, a ragtag team of softball players - mainly comprised of men from Moorestown Bible Church - entered the front gate of Leesburg (now Bayside) State Prison in Leesburg, New Jersey. It was never my intention to focus exclusively on prison ministry. In fact, not having received so much as a speeding ticket, it was the furthest thing from my mind. Instead, I was planning to mirror the Christian Nine, playing softball in local recreation leagues in the hopes of witnessing to other teams. However, God had something entirely different – and greater – in mind.

A month or so before our first game, a gentleman from my parents' church gave me a call. Having heard from my mother that I was starting an evangelistic softball team, he gave me the name of someone to contact in order to set up a game. The contact's name was Nick Barbetta and he was

the Senior Chaplain for the Philadelphia Prison System.
By now you may be wondering why, if Nick was my
original prison contact, we played our first game at
Leesburg. Well, the answer is simple. I ran ahead of God.

Actually, in my exuberance to start witnessing, I started to
grow restless when I hadn't heard back from Nick within
what I considered to be a reasonable amount of time. And
so, I listened to some bad advice and tried a different
approach. I placed a direct call to Rich Sforza, the
Recreation Supervisor for the Philadelphia Prison System.
By the time I got off the phone with Rich, we had a game
scheduled and I couldn't have been more pleased. That is,
until I received a follow-up call from Nick.

"Well, Dale, you're in," Nick said. "But I want you to know
that I don't appreciate the way you went about it," he added.

The "spiritual high" that I had experienced just hours before
instantly gave way to a feeling of intense remorse. Nick
then gently but firmly lectured me on the proper way of
doing things within the prison system. He graciously
accepted my apology and before signing off, even wished
our team and me well.

I still feel badly about acting like a "bull in a china shop"
that day, but I had learned a valuable lesson about prison
procedures and proper protocol. I had also gained a
valuable friend. Despite my youthful mistake, Nick agreed
to become a charter member of our advisory council and
has served as the keynote speaker at two of our annual
banquets. To this day, whenever I have a specific question
or a special need, Nick is only a phone call away.

Of course, that still doesn't explain why we played our first game at Leesburg instead of at one of the Philadelphia prisons. Simply put, before we could play our game in Philadelphia, we managed to schedule another game at Leesburg. And that's how we found ourselves at their front gate on a gorgeous Saturday afternoon in June 1987.

As I said earlier, our first softball team was made up of men from Moorestown Bible Church with a smattering of guys I knew from high school or other church teams. Our uniforms were comprised of white t-shirts with red trim and the name "Saints" spelled across our chests in lower case letters. Most of us wore jeans or sweatpants, while a few players still had their baseball pants from college. In his early fifties, pitcher Henry Koch wore cut-off shorts and sneaks.

What that first team lacked in style or ability, they more than made up for with heart. I am forever indebted to them for adopting my dream as their own, and for adding flesh to my vision. As I've said many times since, "no one would come out to watch Dale Glading play softball by himself." Without these pioneers – and the scores of dedicated missionary athletes who have followed in their footsteps – there wouldn't be a Saints Prison Ministry today.

And so, please allow me to honor these original Saints players for leading the way:

> Henry Koch – pitcher
> Jim Korth - 1st base
> Mark Kaiser – 2nd base
> David Scott – shortstop
> Tom Schurr – 3rd base

Steve Hastie – left field
Phil Smith – left center field
Duane Fischer – right center field
Walt Cannon – right field
Bob Bartosz – catcher
Dave Beppler – designated hitter

If memory serves me, Lou Juhlmann also played for us that first year as did Pete Dempsey. Bill Reiss, Frank "Deac" DeConcini and Bob Hellyer all started their Saints careers in 1988 and were soon joined by Lex DiNick, Jeff Lex and Jeff Marthins. And how could I forget Dave "the Hammer" Storms, our first legitimate power hitter, who was named our team MVP for the first of three times in 1990.

But back to June 6, 1987 for a moment. Not knowing what to expect, we planned on the unexpected. That meant bringing an overstocked equipment bag complete with bases. However, you should have seen the expression on the officer's face when we tried to bring in spikes to fasten down those bases!

Despite our naiveté, we played a competitive game that day, losing in the final inning. Most importantly, eight prisoners made professions of faith in Jesus Christ. While the finish line may not have been crossed, The South Jersey Saints were finally out of the starting blocks.

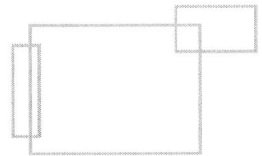

"Charlie Ashman Won't Let Me!"
June – September 1987

"But Jesus said to him, 'No one, having put his hand to the plow, and looking back, is fit for the kingdom of God."
Luke 9:62 (NKJV)

Up until June 6, 1987, I had only led one person to the Lord, face to face. Now, in a single day of playing ball and preaching God's Word in prison, eight men had trusted Christ as Savior.

I knew that I was "on" to something, but still didn't view the Saints as a full-time vocation let alone my future career. I guess that's why my family and I loaded up our car and drove to Martha's Vineyard just three months later.

There are few places as beautiful as Cape Cod in September. The summer crowds have gone and it's the perfect place for a young couple and their infant daughter to get away for a much-needed vacation.

Deanna and I had booked an efficiency apartment for the week and spent much of our time sightseeing around the island. Despite a nasty head cold, I was really enjoying my time alone with my two favorite girls. The sleepy pace of Edgartown in the fall also allowed me to catch up on some reading.

The book that God had me reading at that particular time was an autobiography entitled, *The Apples in a Seed.* It was written by Charles Ashman, the founder of Camp Ha-lu-wa-sa, a Christian camp in Hammonton, New Jersey. For those not familiar with Ha-lu-wa-sa, it stands for Hallelujah, what a Savior!

Well, the main premise of Charlie's book is that you can look at an apple seed and see one of two things. You can either see just that, a single apple seed, or you can see an entire apple orchard. Simply put, it's a matter of perspective. Are you willing to trust God and see things through His eyes? If so, the potential in a single apple seed is virtually unlimited.

Charlie applied this same spiritual principle in his life when he first visited what was to become Camp Ha-lu-wa-sa in the 1950's. Others may have seen a swamp in the middle of the Jersey Pine Barrens, but God gave Charlie the eyes to envision a Christian camp. Today, thousands of kids have come to Christ because of Charlie's faithfulness to his God-given vision.

I believe that my reading Charlie's book on this particular trip was all part of God's master plan for my life. You see, on the way home from Martha's Vineyard, I had an appointment scheduled at Springfield College in Springfield, Massachusetts. My intention was to secure a position as a graduate assistant and to earn my Master's degree in Recreation Management.

However, as I turned the pages of Charlie's book, God began to speak to me. I knew in my heart that if I left New

Jersey to attend Springfield College, the Saints ministry would die on the vine. It would never realize it's God-given potential.

And so, somewhat unexpectedly, I found myself standing in a phone booth in Edgartown, Massachusetts, calling the Recreation Department at Springfield College. I don't remember my exact words to the folks there as I cancelled my appointment, but I might as well have told them the truth…*"Charlie Ashman won't let me!"*

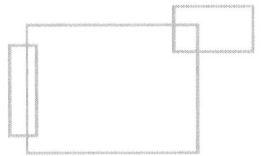

How Firm a Foundation
October 1987 – July 1990

*"For no other foundation can anyone lay than that which
is laid, which is Jesus Christ."*
I Corinthians 3:11 (NKJV)

Now that I had decided to stay in New Jersey and see what
God had in store for the Saints, there were some pressing
matters to which I had to attend. First, we had to see that
The South Jersey Saints was properly incorporated. And so,
with the help of Bill Hyland, a Christian attorney, we filed
for incorporation in 1988 and received our tax-exempt
status the following year. Bill has remained a dear friend of
our ministry and continues to provide us with pro bono legal
services to this day.

One of the requirements for incorporation was to form a
Board of Trustees. Not knowing any better, we opted to
hold our first such election in the visiting room at Leesburg
State Prison following a softball game that first season. I
was elected President and Jim Korth, my friend and pastor,
was chosen as Vice President. Rounding out our first board
were Tom Schurr, Secretary, and Dave Beppler, Treasurer.
Within a year, Tom would become President as my job title
was changed to Executive Director and David Scott would
take over as Treasurer. Shortly thereafter, Jim Korth was
elevated to Senior Pastor at our church and as a result, Steve
Hastie assumed the reins as Vice President of the ministry.

Another requirement for incorporation was a constitution and bylaws. Once again, Jim Korth aided in this process, but the main architect of these documents was Larry Lufburrow.

Larry and his wife Millie were the first residents of The Village at Wiley. I met them a few days after they moved in and quickly developed a deep friendship with both of them. In fact, Larry became my spiritual mentor, and both he and Millie continue to be "adopted" grandparents to our three children.

Because Larry had served on numerous mission boards and was the former Dean of Students at Philadelphia College of Bible, he proved invaluable during the formative years of the Saints. In addition to providing wise counsel, Larry served two terms on our board of trustees. He remains a man of few words, but like the old E.F. Hutton commercials, when Larry speaks, people listen!

With a solid foundation laid, it was time to turn our attention towards enhancing the ministry aspects of the Saints. Specifically, I was burdened to see our outreach to prisoners become a year-round endeavor.

Here in the Northeast, softball is at best a seven-month proposition. You can start practicing outdoors in April, or March if the weather is particularly mild. Most seasons end during the dog days of summer, meaning late July or early August. Our Saints softball seasons have evolved over the years to where we play well into September with a postseason crusade in October added for good measure. However, that still leaves the fall and winter months when playing softball in prison isn't an option.

My first thought was to take our softball team and head south at least once a year. Surely there were prisoners in Florida who needed to hear the Good News of Jesus Christ! However, I couldn't get enough players to commit to that idea and so, we decided to launch a second team in a different sport. Since we would be recruiting many of our original softball players to play on this new team, it was important to pick a sport in which they were reasonably proficient. So, just that simply, the Saints Volleyball Team was formed.

Team leaders included captain Scott Iepson and the father-son combination of Gary and Rich Kipp. But while this team was successful in sharing the gospel with prisoners throughout the cold winter months, we soon realized that volleyball had its limitations. Basically, we had to teach the inmates the rudiments of the game before we could compete against them, which made for some rather lopsided matches.

Eventually, it occurred to us that the majority of the prisoners we were ministering to came from the inner-city. Most of them were minorities and they hadn't played much volleyball growing up. No, if we were going to reach inmates for Christ during the off-season, we were going to have do so by playing their favorite sport...basketball.

However, before we could form a Saints basketball team, we had to ask ourselves two critical questions. First, would we be able to deal with the more physical nature of the game? Compared to softball, basketball is a much more demanding sport, played at a high speed with a lot of bumping and shoving going on. Would our players be willing to absorb that kind of punishment without retaliating?

Second, and perhaps more importantly, would we be able to compete on the inmates' level? The Saints ministry had been built upon the premise that earning the inmates' respect athletically was crucial to effectively ministering the gospel to them. Could a group of mostly Caucasian softball players don basketball uniforms and still be an effective witness for Jesus Christ?

Enter Ernie Armstead, all 6'8" of him. Basically, our team's strategy was to play strong defense and to get the ball inside to Ernie. Fortunately, we had a few players who could knock down jumpers from the outside as well, and so we were off and running. In fact, our team went undefeated that first season, although we played only two games.

Such a patchwork offense was O.K. for the short term, but we realized that we would have to do some major recruiting if we were to expand our schedule the following year. Prisons such as the State Correctional Institution in Graterford, Pennsylvania have more than 3,000 inmates to draw from when selecting a team. Imagine having several thousand players trying out for a 12-man squad!

Once again, God answered our need in a way we couldn't have imagined. Tony DiCaro, a sweet-shooting guard who had played collegiately at St. Joseph's University, agreed to join our team. Even better, Tony had a friend who he thought might be interested. When I found out that his friend was Darryl Gladden, I almost fell off my chair!

Darryl was one of the greatest high school basketball players in South Jersey history. He had starred at Kennedy High School in Willingboro before receiving a scholarship to LaSalle University. At LaSalle, Darryl set all kinds of scoring and assist records, and had drawn the attention of a number of professional scouts. It looked like a NBA career was in the offing, until his senior year that is, when he was kicked off the team for a rules violation.

God used this episode in Darryl's life to draw him to salvation. Passed up in the NBA draft because of his background, he went onto a successful career with the Lancaster Lightning of the Continental Basketball Association. Eventually, Darryl retired from the CBA and started a carpet business with his lovely wife, Andrea. However, he still had lots of basketball left in him and God wanted him to use it to lead inmates to Christ.

It's a good thing that Tony and Darryl decided to join our team, because we were about to receive a phone call from a prison chaplain in Florida that would change the direction of the Saints ministry.

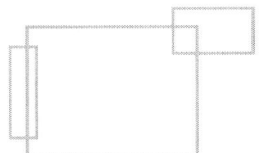

The Next Time Will Be the First Time
August 1990 – February 1992

"But you shall receive power when the Holy Spirit has come upon you; and you shall be witnesses to Me in Jerusalem, and in all Judea and Samaria, and to the end of the earth." Acts 1:8 (NKJV)

In the summer of 1990, we were in the midst of our fourth softball season. After playing just five games our first year, our schedule had grown to include several dozen prisons throughout New Jersey, Southeastern Pennsylvania and Delaware. It was now time to broaden our horizons.

Chaplain Bungo was responsible for the spiritual welfare of the men at the Mercer County Prison in Mercer, Pennsylvania. Unlike Graterford, Frackville and Camp Hill however, Mercer was a solid eight-hour drive from our office in Moorestown, New Jersey. So, when Chaplain Bungo called me out of the blue to ask if our softball team would be willing to visit his institution, I was taken by surprise.

After consulting with some key players, I called Chaplain Bungo back and accepted his gracious invitation. And so, the first Saints crusade was born!

That first crusade was over a long weekend, meaning that we left in the wee hours on Friday morning and got back late on Sunday night. In between, we played six games, winning five, and conducted a chapel service. We also spoke and sang at a church in Hollidaysburg, Pennsylvania on the way home.

I have many memories of that first crusade, some humorous and some rather poignant. One of the more comical memories involves the motel where we stayed. Trying to save money, we opted for a small establishment on the outskirts of town. I'm not saying that it was run down, but the management took great pride in advertising the fact that they offered "free parking."

Our first-ever prison chapel service was especially moving and our team gave a good accounting of itself on the playing field as well. We swept a doubleheader on Friday evening against a Christian team and then beat them twice more on Saturday morning. Now that we were bone-tired, it was time to play two more games that afternoon …against their undefeated varsity team!

We were told that Mercer's varsity squad had a 26-game winning streak and in our first game, they proved just how good they were. However, led by the inspired play of third baseman Dave Storms, we rallied to win the second game of our doubleheader.

The only "downer" of the trip was arriving at Grace Bible Church in Hollidaysburg the following morning and discovering that their senior pastor had suffered a stroke the day before. Naturally, the entire congregation was still in shock and there was a lot of turmoil surrounding the worship service. We did our best to present the Saints ministry that morning, but despite being given a warm welcome, it was still a little awkward.

Miraculously, 45 inmates made professions of faith on that first crusade. Because of this success, we were now open to playing and ministering wherever God would have us to go. And we wouldn't have to wait long to find out where that would be.

In the fall of 1991, I received another phone call from a prison chaplain, this time from Florida. Chaplain John Strickland of the Lawtey Correctional Institution wanted to know when would we be making our next trip to Florida.

"The next time will be the first time," I remember telling him. However, after consulting with our board of trustees, we decided to accept his invitation as well. Once again, God was forcing us out of our comfort zone and expanding our ministry horizons.

My experience as a travel agent came into play as I had to make both air and hotel reservations for our team. Then I crossed my fingers and prayed that enough players would be willing to go to field a competitive team.

I shouldn't have worried however, as God had already handpicked a group of talented players to accompany me to Florida. Far more importantly, they were all going for the right reason – to share the Good News of Jesus Christ. Basketball was secondary.

Chaplain Strickland met us at the Jacksonville airport and drove us to our hotel in his church van. For the next four days, he was to be our constant companion, escorting us from prison to prison. In fact, he and his godly wife insisted on washing our team's sweaty uniforms every night. Rarely have I encountered a man with such a servant's heart as John Strickland.

Like our inaugural softball crusade, I have many fond memories of that early basketball crusade. Our first game was on Thursday evening at Lawtey, and Don Conner hit seven three-pointers including a half court shot at the buzzer. After the game, he was mobbed by inmates comparing him to Larry Bird and asking for his autograph.

At the North Florida Reception Center in Lake Butler, we were told that the inmate team featured three players who stood seven feet tall. There was an audible buzz in the gym as we took the floor with everyone predicting a lopsided game. They were right – but not in the way they expected - as we scored the first 21 points of the game to win going away. Darryl Gladden led our team, as he did the entire trip, with 35 points.

Florida State Prison is a maximum-security institution in Starke. In 20 years of prison ministry, it is one of the few institutions where I have felt uneasy. However, God granted our players His peace as we split a doubleheader. I had the privilege of preaching at FSP and the experience was so monumental that I can remember my message to this day.

Our final game on that crusade was versus a neighborhood team called "The Running Rebels". Chaplain Strickland had arranged the game as a community outreach and, despite being physically spent from our grueling schedule, our players eagerly accepted the challenge. The game went into overtime – just what a tired team *didn't* need – but we dug deep and pulled out another victory.

The following morning we returned to Lawtey to conduct a worship service at Chaplain Strickland's invitation. Rev. David McMurray brought such an impassioned message that I broke down crying. In fact – almost 15 years later - I still recall that he spoke on Ruth and Boaz. "Pastor Dave" gave another sermon on Noah during one of our early softball crusades to the Altoona area that also left me in tears. What a gifted preacher!

We concluded our first-ever Florida Crusade with a winning record. However, the only victories that mattered on this or any crusade were the 90 inmates who made decisions for Christ. No wonder our players returned home physically exhausted, but spiritually rejuvenated.

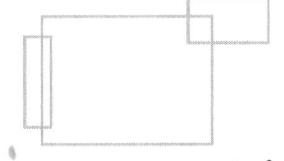

"Don't You Even *Think* About Going Full Time!"

March 1992 – December 1993

"For the gifts and the calling of God are irrevocable."
Romans 11:29 (NKJV)

I have told many people over the years that Deanna's heavenly rewards will be far greater than mine and I mean it. Aside from the obvious – her having to put up with me for more than 20 years – I was the one whom God called to start The Saints Prison Ministry, not her. That is why I believe that her rewards will be so much greater, because I simply did what I *had* to do. Deanna did what she *chose* to do.

And so, while she was initially supportive as I pursued my calling, she also had some rather forceful words of caution for me.

"Don't you even *think* of going full time," Deanna told me on more than one occasion.

You see, as the Saints ministry had grown, so had my responsibilities. I had gone from being a volunteer to serving as Executive Director on a part time basis. Gradually, my Saints hours increased as I began to work four 10-hour days at Wiley. The following year I negotiated with Gary Gilmore to only work 3 1/2 days at Wiley in lieu of a raise. Now, Deanna could see the handwriting on the wall and she was worried.

Being as thickheaded as I am, I haven't learned as much as I should have during our two decades of marriage. However, one of the things I have picked up on is that women, in general, want security. They want to know where they are going to live and where they are going to raise their family. And they also want to know where the money is going to come from to support that family.

Deanna had seen enough during the first five years of the ministry to realize that paychecks weren't always guaranteed. Sometimes they were late and sometimes we were paid in "installments". Dealing with late or partial paychecks from a part-time job was one thing, but how could she be expected to maintain a family budget if I were to go full time with the Saints?

In January 1993, Gary Gilmore notified all of the department heads at Wiley that he wanted to meet with us. Since he had become the administrator there, his practice had been to meet with his senior staff early each year to set goals for their respective departments. And so, I went about the business of putting together my goals for the Recreation Department.

However, as I did so, I felt a certain uneasiness. I couldn't quite put my finger on it, no matter how hard I tried. Finally, it dawned on me. I was having trouble setting my departmental goals because I knew that I wouldn't be there to see them fully realized!

So, when my meeting with Gary began, I told him that I needed to tell him something first. "I don't think I'll be here long enough to reach any of these goals," I said. "God is calling me to go full time, probably by the end of this year."

Gary just stared at me in disbelief and then began to chuckle. "That's so funny," he replied. "Before our meeting, I realized that things are getting so busy around here that I can't have you only working 3 1/2 days a week. I need you to go back to working full time and I was trying to think how to tell you that. Basically, I was going to say that you had to choose between Wiley and the Saints."

I couldn't hold back my laughter either. "Well, it's pretty clear that God has already made that decision for me," I said. I don't know who felt a greater sense of relief, Gary or me.

Eleven years earlier, at Haddon Heights Baptist Church, I had committed my life to full time Christian service. Now, God was making good on my promise...and His.

Even now, it amazes me to think that not only did God call me to start the Saints ministry, but He also predetermined the exact moment for me to go full time. He had clearly been working in Gary's heart at the same time he had been working in mine.

With Gary's blessing, I spent my final 10 months at Wiley on deputation. Sure, I continued to carry out my responsibilities as a department head, but I also sent out support letters to everyone I knew. As money came in, I placed it into an escrow account. By the end of the year, I was about 90% supported and had enough to live on for the next 12 months.

The only disadvantage to announcing my impending departure from Wiley so early was having to console the dozens of residents who stopped me in the halls to wish me well. "We're going to miss you," they would always say. It was gratifying to say the least, but also eerily reminiscent of attending one's own funeral, extended over a 10-month period.

Needless to say, I was excited and somewhat relieved when December 31st finally rolled around. The staff and residents at Wiley threw me a very nice farewell party and then it was over. After the security of working - and for a time, living - at Wiley for the past 11 years, I was finally leaving the nest. I could only hope that God had adequately prepared me for what was to lie ahead.

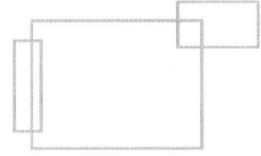

In Satan's Crosshairs
January – March 1994

"For I consider that the sufferings of this present time are not worthy to be compared with the glory which shall be revealed in us." Romans 8:18 (NKJV)

On my first day as a full time employee of The Saints Prison Ministry, I received a call from Dave Shropshire, our new board president. "Just calling to wish you well," Dave said cheerfully.

Dave is the kind of guy who seems perpetually happy. He is a successful businessman, having founded his own traffic-engineering firm, Shropshire Associates, in Lumberton. However, you would never know it by Dave's easygoing demeanor and his down to earth manner. Add to that mix a wonderful wife, Lynne, and two great kids, Cris and Allie, and you know why I've often said that I want to be Dave Shropshire when I grow up. I guess it's that "growing up" part that keeps holding me back.

In any case, my first two weeks on the job couldn't have gone better and I was basking in the glow of God's calling. As I've told many people over the years, I felt like I had stumbled upon my own fate. I was doing exactly what God wanted me to do - the very purpose, I believed, for which I was created.

Yes, things were going extremely well...until January 20, 1994.

That evening, shortly before bedtime, our three children were enjoying some ice cream around the kitchen table. We had been blessed to buy a real "fixer upper" in Pennsauken a few years earlier. A three-bedroom Cape Cod, it didn't matter to us that it was situated just 12 blocks from the Camden border.

So, there they were, our three most precious "possessions", eating what our son Christopher has always referred to as "the green kind", chocolate chip mint. Deanna and I were in the living room watching TV when Bethany called us with some alarm in her voice.

"Christopher is acting weird," were her exact words. I will remember them to the day I die. It was her way of saying that her little brother was suffering a massive stroke.

Christopher Mark Glading was born on February 20, 1991. He must have been in a hurry to make his debut, because Deanna was in labor with him for less than 30 minutes. Aside from a slight heart murmur, which he grew out of, he appeared to be a normal baby. A normal baby, that is, with a terrible temper.

When Chris didn't get his way, he had a habit of banging his head on the floor. Hard. Over and over again until it bruised. Our pediatrician told us that he would stop when it hurt him. Well, apparently, Chris had a high tolerance for pain. In fact, the pictures from his first birthday party show him with a large knot on his forehead.

At 18 months, Chris experienced a seizure of unknown origin. We called an ambulance and he was taken to Cooper Hospital in Camden. A few weeks later, we were sitting in a pediatric neurosurgeon's office at Children's Hospital in Philadelphia, being told that his seizure wasn't a seizure after all. It was a TIA, otherwise known as a mini-stroke.

Dr. Leslie Sutton diagnosed Chris with Moya-Moya Syndrome, a genetic disease in which the blood vessels in the brain "occlude" or close off. It is extremely rare, with only 10,000 known cases worldwide. There is no known cause for Moya-Moya and no known cure. Dr. Sutton's advice to us was to wait and see what happened. And so, we did, until January 20, 1994.

As Bethany had said, Chris was indeed "acting weird." He had dropped his spoon, and ice cream was running out his mouth and down his chin. He had a far-off look in his eyes and couldn't speak.

This time, we didn't wait for the ambulance. Deanna and I jumped in the car and rushed him back to Cooper Hospital.

"My son's having a stroke," I told the triage nurse. She gave me a rather patronizing look as if to say that, "two-year olds don't have strokes."

However, having worked at Wiley for almost 11 years – and having witnessed Chris's TIA just months before - I knew all too well what a stroke looked like. Droopy side of the face. Slurred or no speech. Weakness or paralysis along one side of the body. Unfortunately, Chris exhibited all the classic symptoms.

With no treatment available, we were told to take Chris home and monitor him through the night. When his symptoms didn't improve, we made another appointment with Dr. Sutton.

Dr. Sutton confirmed our amateur diagnosis that Chris had indeed suffered a massive stroke. He then told us of a new surgical procedure called EDAS that was being done on an experimental basis. In layman's terms, the surgery involved stripping arteries from the patient's scalp and stitching them onto the surface of his brain in the hope that the brain would "tap" into this new blood supply before its own internal arteries occluded. Basically, it was a race against time with no guarantees.

Although he was familiar with the procedure, Dr. Sutton had never performed it himself. Instead, he told us that there were three places in the world that offered that surgery – Boston, Toronto and Tokyo.

Our first call was to Boston, but the chief of the Pediatric Neurosurgery Department at Children's Hospital was attending an overseas conference. So, we placed a call to his counterpart in Toronto and he cut right to the chase.

"If Chris doesn't have this surgery," he explained, "he will continue to have more and more debilitating strokes until he is completely incapacitated and dies." Before we could absorb the full impact of his words, he added, "but if he has the surgery, he won't have any more strokes."

The choice was clear and so, we placed another call to Children's Hospital in Boston where Dr. Michael Scott was back from his conference. He was unwilling to say that the surgery would prevent future strokes, but agreed that it was Chris' best chance for survival, let alone for a normal life.

On March 8, 1994, Chris underwent eight hours of experimental surgery at Children's Hospital in Boston, four hours on each side of his brain. The day before, I had broken down sobbing in the hospital chapel while he was undergoing an arteriogram. It had suddenly hit me that my little boy might never wake up from the anesthesia.

However, the day of his actual surgery, both Deanna and I felt an overwhelming peace. Perhaps it was the knowledge that so many people were praying for him. Or perhaps it was the knowledge that we had done all we could, and that Chris was now in the hands of a world-renowned surgeon…and a God who loved him far more than we ever could.

Chris came through the surgery without any complications, but we were still not prepared for his appearance when we got to see him in the recovery room. His cute little face was swollen to twice its normal size and his eyes, black and blue, were swollen shut. Until he was about two years old, Chris had been a real "Momma's boy". Recently, however, he had grown much closer to me and so, I got to spend the night with him in ICU.

Today, Chris is 16-years old and attends Baptist Regional School in Haddon Heights. Except for taking aspirin each day to thin his blood, he leads a normal life. Born right-handed, he now uses his left hand to do everything. Chris is a straight "A" student and an exceptional athlete; playing soccer, basketball and baseball depending on the season. To see him catch a ball in the outfield with his left hand, only to whip his glove off and throw the ball back in with the same hand, is a sight to behold.

I have chosen to include this episode in Christopher's life as a testament to his courage and to illustrate a lesson I would just as soon not have learned. Shortly after Chris's stroke, Cecil Gilmore, Jr. pulled me aside and offered some words of wisdom.

"Don't think it's a coincidence that your son had a stroke just 20 days after you went into full time ministry," he said. The inference was clear. I had crossed the line from spectator to combatant as far as spiritual warfare was concerned. Satan wasn't happy with my decision to follow God's call and now, both my family and I were squarely in his crosshairs.

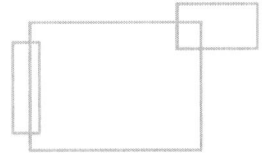

Don't Ever Ask Deac to Pray for the Weather!
June 1987 – Present

"A merry heart does good, like medicine."
Proverbs 17:22 (NKJV)

After composing such an emotional chapter, I need to write something a little "lighter" before I finish this book. My intention is to conclude by covering some of the growing pains – both positive and negative – that the Saints ministry has experienced over its first two decades and then to share my personal vision for the next 20 years.

But first, allow me to share with you some of the more light-hearted moments in Saints history. They are numerous and for some reason, many of them involve Francis "Deac" DeConcini.

Frank DeConcini is one of two people I know who makes me smile when they enter a room. Walt Nesbitt, who has patrolled right-center field for the Saints for a number of years, is the other. Both men fall into the category of "what you see is what you get." As I age – and presumably mature in my Christian faith – I gravitate more and more to such genuinely transparent people.

Deac is the main character in more Saints stories than any

other missionary athlete. A self-effacing player with a solid line-drive swing, he is best known for his off-the-field antics. Along with Marvell Whitley, he is also one of the best storytellers in Saints history. Spend 10 hours a day in a crowded 15-passenger van, and you'll get an idea just how valuable that trait can be.

My favorite "Deac story" involves a game at the State Correctional Institution at Camp Hill, Pennsylvania back in the mid 90's. Camp Hill is located just west of Harrisburg, making it a solid two-hour drive from Moorestown.

On this particular day, the weatherman was calling for rain. We left Moorestown under overcast skies and the clouds continued to thicken as we headed west. However, it was still dry as we entered the prison and made the long walk to the recreation yard.

As we approached the softball field, the recreation director took me aside. "This game is a really big deal for the men here," he began. "They've been looking forward to your visit for months." He went on to say that the game would be videotaped, including the playing of our national anthem.

After warming up, both teams assembled along the baselines for the pre-game ceremony. Sensing that the weather could turn ugly at any moment, the recreation director played his trump card...he asked one of our players to pray. Specifically, he asked Deac to pray that it wouldn't rain.

Obligingly, Deac stepped forward and began to pray in a loud, yet solemn voice. "Dear God," Deac offered, "if it be

Your will, we ask that you hold off the rain." Well, you guessed it. As if on cue, the moment the word "rain" left Deac's lips, the heavens opened up. And it didn't just rain, it poured, in Noah-like proportions.

Somehow, Deac composed himself long enough to finish his prayer. It was a different story however, for my teammates and me. To this day, I can't remember another time when I laughed audibly while someone prayed, but I just couldn't hold it back. My shoulders actually shook as I watched the comical scene unfold. And things only got funnier, because now it was time for the Star Spangled Banner.

The honor of playing our national anthem had fallen to an inmate trumpet player, who had been practicing for weeks for just this occasion. However, as the rains cascaded down on the assembled teams, the recreation director kept urging him to play faster and faster. Soaked to the skin, with water pouring off his instrument, his solo sounded more like "Pop Goes the Weasel" than "O Say Can You See."

Remarkably, as soon as he finished playing, the game went on as planned. After playing for five innings in tropical storm-like conditions, the rain let up and the sun actually broke through the clouds. I think I can speak for both teams when I say that it was a lot of fun sloshing through the mud that day. However, my most vivid memory will always be of the Lord answering Deac's prayer with a torrential downpour. Whoever said that God doesn't have a sense of humor?

Another Saints story that has been retold countless times also took place at Camp Hill. However, this time Hugh Dwyer was the protagonist.

Hugh is one of the most popular softball players to ever wear a Saints uniform. Despite his relative youth, he has served as a team captain and assistant manager for many years. A talented pitcher and clutch hitter, Hugh is known to his teammates as the "Gamemeister." He earned this moniker by organizing trivia games, which have helped us to pass hundreds of hours in the Saints van.

On this particular May afternoon, the sun was shining brightly. In fact, it was unseasonably hot, with the temperatures soaring into the mid 90's. Being short-handed, I inserted Hugh into the starting lineup at third base. I knew it wasn't his usual position, but I was confident that his youthful reflexes would serve him well.

In the very first inning, a left-handed batter sliced a line drive down the third baseline. I guess Hugh was expecting him to pull the ball instead, because he was a little late in getting his glove up. As a result, the ball careened off his glove and directly into his face.

I don't recall whether Hugh picked up the ball and completed the play. What I do remember, however, is that he started sifting through the infield dirt for something else – his two front teeth. Along with a couple of others, they had been knocked out of Hugh's mouth and onto the base path.

Hugh eventually found most of his teeth and we soaked them in milk obtained from the prison kitchen. Following our doubleheader, we then spent several hours at a local orthodontist's office before heading home exhausted from the heat.

And so, whereas Tony Bennett may have "left his heart in San Francisco", Hugh Dwyer left his teeth at Camp Hill.

Not every prison story involves one of our softball players. On a long trip to Connecticut, two of our basketball players were the principal characters in yet another chapter in Saints folklore.

Our team had played a series of three-on-three games that morning at the Webster Correctional Institution in Cheshire. We were short-handed that day, too, so much so that I actually had to suit up. After "enjoying" prison food for lunch, an inmate choir ministered to us in music.

Now that we were both tired and stuffed, it was time to play a full-court game versus Webster's varsity squad. As you can imagine, we fell behind early and trailed throughout the game. Things got worse when Bob Newcomb, our 6'6" center, sprained his ankle and had to come out.

But instead of giving up, our exhausted players started to rally. Gradually, we cut into Webster's once substantial lead. However, down by eight points with just 10 seconds left, it was apparently a case of too little, too late. Things still looked grim, even after Don Conner banked in a long three-pointer.

Against all odds, we then stole the in-bound pass and scored a quick lay-up. The crowd went crazy, but the fact remained that we still trailed by three with less than two seconds on the clock.

Webster was determined not to turn the ball over again under their own basket and so, their in-bounder threw the ball the length of the court. There it was intercepted by Rick Moore, another one of our 6'6" centers. In the same motion, Rick heaved the ball back in the general direction of our basket. It smacked hard off the backboard and then, wonder of wonders, dropped straight in!

Miraculously, we had scored eight points in 10 seconds! As Rick's desperation shot swished through the net, our bench erupted in sheer disbelief. No one was more excited than Bob Newcomb, who forgot for a minute about his injury. Bob leapt into the air with both arms raised over his head. It wasn't until he was airborne that he realized that the law of gravity would soon take over and he would come crashing down on that painfully swollen ankle. Thankfully, the roar of the crowd drowned out Bob's groan as he landed on his injured foot.

Don Conner figured prominently in our Webster comeback. He is also one of a handful of Saints missionary athletes who has played for more than one of our sports teams. Basketball may be Don's first love, but he is an immensely talented softball player, too.

Our teams have played and ministered at Sing Sing many times over the years. Located in Ossining, New York, Sing Sing is one of the oldest prisons in the country, having been in continuous use since 1825. At one time, it housed New York State's electric chair, making it an ideal venue to film one of Jimmy Cagney's movies, *Angels with Dirty Faces*. Situated on the Hudson River, Sing Sing is also where the phrases, "the big house" and being sent "up the river" were coined.

Like many New York State prisons, Sing Sing's varsity team prefers to play fast-pitch softball. Don is our best and fastest pitcher and so, he got the starting nod that day. However, what stands out in my mind isn't how he pitched that evening, but rather his at-bat halfway through the game.

The two teams were locked in a low-scoring pitcher's duel until about the fourth inning, when Don came to bat for the second time. "D.C." was using a titanium bat that day, which has since been outlawed for safety reasons by most softball associations.

As the pitch came in, Don swung as hard as his 6'5" frame would allow. The ball literally exploded off his bat and started on a long, high trajectory towards the wall in left-center field. We had been told before the game that no one in Sing Sing's 180-year history had ever hit a ball out of the prison yard. And no wonder, with a 30-foot high concrete wall in left topped by a 10-foot barbed wire fence.

However, this was no ordinary night and Don is no ordinary player. His ball easily cleared the wall, the fence and the street outside the prison. It then ricocheted off a 10-story building, approximately 2/3 of the way up. Simply put, it was the longest and hardest-hit ball I have ever seen.

Our players didn't know how to react. I can remember hugging Glenn Hastie, who was standing in the on-deck circle. Other players laughed uncontrollably or just shook their heads in amazement. The inmate spectators couldn't believe it either and simply cheered as loudly as they could. All the while, Don jogged around the bases, shrugging his shoulders as if to say, "What's the big deal?" Well, it was a big deal Don, because the inmates at Sing Sing are still talking about it almost 15 years later!

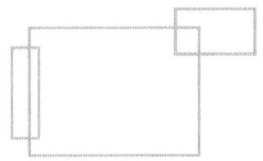

Growing Pains
February 1994 – December 2006

"Call to Me, and I will answer you, and show you great and mighty things, which you do not know."
Jeremiah 33:3 (NKJV)

As our outreach extended to prisons well beyond the Delaware Valley and even the Tri-State area, it became necessary for our board to consider a name change. "The South Jersey Saints" had served us well during the ministry's infancy, but now that God was expanding our horizons it was time for a corporate name that reflected such growth.

After much deliberation and prayer, we selected "The Saints Prison Ministry". Once again, Bill Hyland took care of the legal filings and Dave Storms, our board vice president at the time, designed a new ministry logo.

Around the same time, we realized that both our office and our paid staff needed to grow as well. We had already graduated from the basement of our house in Pennsauken to the unfinished balcony of the Moorestown Bible Church. Gradually, and with the church's blessing, our operations expanded to include the entire balcony and the former youth room. Along with the additional office space came some very welcome storage areas under the eaves of the church.

As I mentioned, it was no longer possible for me to handle the day-to-day operations of the ministry single-handedly. For the first 10 years, I had been The Saints lone employee. Had it not been for volunteers such as Elaine Stephens, Karen Scott, Doug Samuel and June Glading, I don't know how we could have survived.

Elaine has been with me since the very beginning of the Saints ministry. Whether she was called by God to join me or simply felt sympathy for an over-worked, under-qualified young man, I'm not sure. Knowing Elaine, I suspect it was both.

Over the past 20 years, Elaine has been a real jack-of-all-trades – grading Bible studies, coordinating bulk mailings and performing whatever general office work needed to be done. She is truly one of God's choice servants and our Volunteer of the Year award is rightfully named for her.

Karen Scott is the wife of Dave, one of our original softball players. While David was busy playing shortstop and serving on our board of trustees, Karen maintained our financial records during those early years. Meanwhile, my brother-in-law Doug Samuel published our first newsletter and continued to help with its production until he relocated to Florida.

Finally, my mother June has served the Saints with distinction for going on two decades. In addition to helping with bulk mailings and grading Bible studies, she is best known for single-handedly overseeing our birthday card ministry. Sending hand-signed birthday greetings to nearly 25,000 prisoners every year is a monumental undertaking.

However, no other aspect of the Saints ministry receives as many letters of appreciation from inmates.

When the ministry's bookkeeping needs increased to the point where we had to add paid staff, Jeff Marthins was our first hire. "Mr. Tastykake" as Jeff is known, did a fine job for several years before his responsibilities at the Tasty Baking Company forced him to relinquish his position with the Saints. And yet, Jeff remains extremely active as a missionary athlete with more than 16 years of dedicated service.

In the late 1990's, I began to pray specifically for one thing...an Elisha. Not that I believed that I was in the "same league" as Elijah or that I was the only one who hadn't bowed his knee to Baal. I simply needed a right-hand man with whom to share the blessings and burdens of full-time ministry.

As God had done years before when he called me to leave my job at the Wiley Mission, He found another willing servant in Frank Zeidler, Jr. Frank's background was equally humble as he supported his family by servicing kitchen equipment, mostly commercial dishwashers. And yet, God saw Frank's heart and once again, confounded this world's wisdom by handpicking him to be my friend and closest confidant. Today, Frank serves as our Associate Director and is fully capable of assuming the ministry's reins should God call me elsewhere or call me home.

In June 2002, God brought to fruition another piece of the Saints puzzle. We had long been concerned about what happened to the men we ministered to – after their release.

Would they make it "on the outside" or would they fall through the cracks and quickly return to prison?

Nationally, an estimated 75% of all inmates are rearrested within four years of their release. Such a high recidivism rate reflects poorly on the rehabilitation model used by most institutions. However, preliminary findings showed a drastically reduced recidivism rate for Christian inmates, especially for those who were mentored post-release.

But if the Saints were to begin such an aftercare program, where would we start? More importantly, how would we fund our program and whom would we get to oversee it?

The question of funding was temporarily answered by dual grants from the Danellie Foundation and the New Jersey Office of Faith-Based Initiatives. Included in those grants were monies to hire a full-time Director of Transitional Services.

After interviewing a number of qualified candidates, we finally settled on Minister Keith McCrea. I can still see the surprise in Keith's face when I told him that having served time in prison didn't disqualify him, but rather it was a prerequisite for the job!

Keith has a remarkable testimony. A former drug addict and alcoholic, he was in and out (mostly in) a series of state and federal prisons for almost 20 years. Miraculously, Keith came to Christ while incarcerated, and has since dedicated his life to helping other ex-offenders transition successfully back into society.

Despite serving in prison ministry for almost 20 years, I can still be scammed by even a novice con man. Thankfully, Keith is much more street-smart. More than once, I have heard him tell an ex-offender, "What do you mean running that scam? I invented that scam!"

A year after launching our Transitional Services program, we had registered a microscopic recidivism rate of just over 3%. Unfortunately, that number rose to almost 10% following Keith's stroke in November 2004. However, after his return from a medical leave of absence, the Saints' recidivism rate dropped below 8% and has remained there ever since. That means that only 11 of our first 158 clients have re-offended, most of them for minor parole violations.

Call it tough love if you will, but Keith and his program have shown that ministering to the "whole man" results in far fewer ex-offenders returning to prison. In other words, we must address a man's spiritual needs without neglecting his physical and emotional ones. Just feeding or housing him isn't enough; we must also treat his addiction. And most importantly, we must introduce him to the Only One who can heal his spirit and save his soul. After all, isn't that what prison ministry is all about?

In September 2005, the Saints "spun off" our Transitional Services Program into a new entity. Lives in Transition (or L.I.T. Services) is now it's own nonprofit corporation. However, it remains an affiliate of The Saints Prison Ministry and despite Minister McCrea's departure in September 2006, L.I.T. continues to offer services such as food, clothing, transportation, phone cards and toiletry kits for recently released ex-offenders.

Another landmark in Saints history was the establishing of a branch office in Colorado Springs. We conducted a softball crusade to the "Centennial State" in August 2003, with fantastic results. In fact, our team was so well-received that following our first game at the Crowley County Correctional Facility, I was called into the warden's office. Fearing that I was going to be reprimanded for something my team or I had done, I entered rather sheepishly, painfully aware that my dirty cleats were soiling his spotless carpet.

"Mr. Glading," he began as he extended his hand, "that was the best program we have ever had at this institution. Tell me when you and your team can come back."

In disbelief, I stared once again at my cleats and then looked up at the warden. "Three years, maybe four," I stammered before adding, "or maybe five. You see, we simply receive more invitations from prisons across the country than we can possibly accommodate. And so, we keep a pending file and accept these invitations on a first-come, first-served basis."

Fortunately, while we were in Colorado, board president Bob Hellyer and I stayed behind one day for a series of meetings with other ministry leaders. One such meeting was with a representative from the Navigators. As God would have it, the gentleman we met with brought along an intern who was so impressed with our ministry that he went home and shared the concept with his father. "Coincidentally", his dad was a soccer coach who also managed a soccer store in the area. Within days of our return home, John Bryant was on the phone with Bob, laying the groundwork for what is now the Western Branch of The Saints Prison Ministry.

The Saints took another major step forward when we accepted the merger of Jericho Ministries in September 2006. Jericho was founded in the mid-1980's by Rev. Dave Ramsey and Rev. Irene Cox. For more than 25 years, these prison ministry pioneers, along with a host of dedicated volunteers, conducted Bible studies and chapel services in correctional institutions throughout the Garden State. Coupled with our Bible Correspondence School, which boasts an enrollment of 2,500 inmate students, the Jericho merger will allow us to disciple prisoners face-to-face for the very first time. It is our sincere hope that this comprehensive discipleship model will serve as a blueprint for the other 22 states where the Saints currently minister.

Unfortunately, not all of the growing pains the Saints have gone through have been positive ones. Only time will tell whether they were necessary for our long-term success, or simply the result of our best intentions gone awry. I think that most Christians have unrealistic expectations of parachurch ministries and the people who run them. The truth be told, we are imperfect jars of clay more prone to sinful tendencies and human error than many of us are willing to admit. However, God in His grace continues to use us in His great kingdom-building work.

Among these relatively minor but not-so-pleasant experiences have been divisions over doctrinal positions, particularly regarding the issues of separation and spiritual gifts. Personality conflicts have also emerged on the playing field and in the boardroom. Some trustees have urged us to move forward in faith while others have wanted us to exercise more fiscal restraint. And yet, despite our "humanity", God has remained faithful to the Saints for almost 20 years. Thankfully, He shows no signs of withholding His future blessings either.

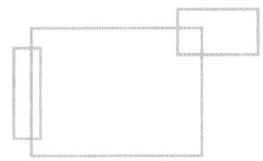

More Van Stories
1987-Present

"You shall teach them to your children, speaking of them
when you sit in your house, when you walk by the way,
when you lie down, and when you rise up."
Deuteronomy 11:19

Before my concluding chapter in which I share my vision
for the Saints future, I want to include a few more "van
stories". I hope that they bring a smile to your face, a tear
to your eye and praise to your lips. As the hymn writer
states, "What a mighty God we serve!"

His name is Rodolfo Jimenez, but everyone calls him
"Tote". Born in Guadalajara, Mexico and educated at Word
of Life in Argentina, Tote came to the United States to
marry Debbie Carter. They had met at Word of Life and a
courtship soon followed.

Arriving in the U.S., Tote performed a series of part time
jobs, but his heart's desire was to serve God on the mission
field. Specifically, he and Debbie wanted to use their
language skills to witness for Christ.

I first met Tote at his home church, Grace Bible Church in
Barrington, New Jersey. I was impressed by his sincerity
and invited him to attend an upcoming softball game at the
Federal Correctional Institution at Fort Dix. Tote gladly

accepted and even translated our gospel message that day. However, it was at an indoor soccer game at the Low Security Correctional Institution in Allenwood, Pennsylvania that I began to realize what an asset he could be to The Saints Prison Ministry.

At Allenwood, one of our players greeted the spectators and a second player then shared his personal testimony. Finally, Tote took the microphone and introduced himself with these words. "Hello, my name is Tote Jimenez and I am from Guadalajara, Mexico." No sooner had he uttered the word "Mexico" than the entire gymnasium erupted in applause. That quickly, the predominantly Latino inmate population had bonded with Tote and they sat transfixed throughout his message. As I recall, 25 men trusted Christ that day, in part because they had heard the gospel preached in their native language.

There have been scores of great gospel messages preached at the more than 1,700 prison games our teams have played since 1987. However, several stand out in my mind to this day and one of them was delivered by Roland "Bud" Collins.

Bud hates it when I say this, but he is arguably the greatest softball player in Saints history (got you again, Bud!) Powerfully built, Bud has hit hundreds of home runs in his Saints career. He is also a gifted outfielder with a strong arm and blazing speed.

And yet, what sets Bud apart is his childlike faith and transparency. A recovering alcoholic and drug addict, Bud doesn't pull any punches when sharing his testimony. However, he hadn't preached the gospel in prison until our first South Carolina Crusade in 2000.

I don't remember whether Bud had asked me for the opportunity or if I had simply scheduled him to speak that day at the Goodman Correctional Institution. What I do recall is how anxious he was. So much so, in fact, that he had asked the entire team to pray for him.

As the final out was recorded, the inmates gathered in a grove of trees to listen to Bud's message. He started strong, but then his voice began to quake with emotion. Comprehending the depth of Christ's forgiveness was one thing. But that day, Bud was equally overwhelmed by God's grace in using him to proclaim the Good News. With tears streaming down both cheeks, Bud gave an impassioned plea for those in attendance to consider the claims of Christ. Under a canopy of trees, more than 30 prisoners responded to the invitation.

Another gospel message that I remember well was delivered by Chaplain Larry Lilly at the Otisville Correctional Facility in upstate New York. Our softball team was to conduct a morning worship service before playing an afternoon doubleheader and "Chap" was the featured speaker. Bob Hellyer was also scheduled to share his personal testimony that morning, but he went a little long. Fearing that Bob was encroaching on Chap's preaching time, I motioned from the back of the room for him to cut it short. However, Bob misinterpreted my signal and thought I was telling him to extend his testimony. And so, by the time Chap strode to the pulpit, his allotted time was down to about eight minutes. I can honestly say that I've never seen anyone go from "zero to 60" in less time, as Chap was pounding the pulpit within a matter of seconds.

Chap and I go back almost 20 years. In fact, he is one of my very best friends. Our first meeting took place at the Sussex Correctional Institution in Georgetown, Delaware where he has served as chaplain for going on 25 years. On our initial visit to his institution, Chap met us in the front gatehouse and introduced himself. This was a real rarity, because most of the time our prison contact is through the recreation department. In fact, up until that point, I don't think we had ever met a prison chaplain. Chap was so impressed with our ministry that day that he joined our softball team the following season and still participates on at least one crusade per year.

Back to that morning chapel service at Otisville for a moment. Between the end of the service and our first softball game, I had a chance to talk to one of the inmates there. I forget his full name, but everyone simply referred to him as "Deacon Hayes". He was one of the leaders in the prison church and I soon found out why.

Sitting outside, gazing at the trees surrounding the ballfield, Deacon Hayes remarked about the beauty of God's creation. "I came from Attica", he said, "where the walls are so high that all you can see is the sky. I hadn't seen a tree in over 10 years until I came here", he added wistfully.

Deacon Hayes went on to tell me an abridged version of his life story. During his period of incarceration, his wife had left him and all three of his children had died, two of them from AIDS. Then a smile broke out on his face that could have only come from the depths of his soul. "But I still have joy", he said reverently. "I still have joy."

Over the years, there have been some equally poignant testimonies shared by our missionary athletes. Three of our softball players - Mark Kaiser, Bob Hellyer and Glenn Hastie – have suffered the tragic loss of a child. Another softball player, Steve Schoch, has a severely handicapped daughter. And yet another softball player, Butch Smith, was abandoned by his father as an infant and raised by an alcoholic mother. But in each of these instances, God has used these apparent tragedies to communicate His love and grace. First, to our players and their families and then, to countless prisoners across the United States and Canada.

Fortunately, for each Saints tragedy experienced, there have been scores of amusing, even hilarious, stories. One such event occurred at the Central Facility in Lorton, Virginia, where the District of Columbia used to house their inmates. Late in the game, Don Conner hit a prodigious home run. However, as he rounded third base, the wind picked up and started to blow his hat off. Don reacted instinctively by grabbing and removing his cap. Immediately, the home plate umpire ruled him out for "showboating". Oh, those prison calls!

Another "van story" involves just that – three rental vans on one of our early Florida crusades. After playing and ministering at the Hendry Correctional Institution in Immokalee, our basketball team enjoyed a late night dinner at a local restaurant. Immokalee is an extremely small town in the middle of nowhere, bordering the Big Cypress Swamp and populated mostly by migrant workers. As I paid the dinner check, I noticed one of our vans pulling out of the parking lot, closely followed by the other two. I was never particularly good at math, but even I know that three minus three equals zero. And so, that meant that I was without a ride back to our hotel.

With time to kill, I bought a newspaper and sat on a curb in the now abandoned parking lot, waiting for someone to realize that I had been left behind. That realization occurred about 45 minutes later when the three vans stopped to refuel and I wasn't there to pay the bill! Sheepishly, one of the vans did a U-turn and I was soon back in the company of my teammates.

However, as stories tend to do, this one quickly took on a life of its own, compliments of Marv Whitley. A master storyteller, his version ends with the van returning to Immokalee just in time to rescue me from a mob of migrant workers. As Marv tells it, I was surrounded by pistol-wielding men who were firing randomly at my feet all the while shouting, "Dance, Gringo, dance!" I have to admit, I prefer Marv's version and have repeated it so many times that I've started to believe it myself.

Coincidentally, that same restaurant in Immokalee was the scene of yet another Saints anecdote. A few years later, we returned for another late-night meal (after all, there are only so may places to eat in Immokalee.) Because of the size of our group, the hostess seated us in a back room and sent a young waitress to take our order. While she was doing so however, one of our players developed a severe charley horse (yes, it was Don Conner...again!) Without warning, he leapt to his feet with a shout, clutching his affected hamstring. As Don hopped around in pain, it was all we could do to keep the unsuspecting waitress from running out of the room!

In addition to our game at Camp Hill where Deac was asked to pray for the weather, our softball teams have played many times in the rain and mud. As recently as our "America's Southwest Crusade" in October 2006, our players got so muddy that we had to use an outdoor spigot to "hose off" before the prison officials would allow us to walk back through their administrative area. I also recall a game in South Carolina where the rain fell so hard that a small stream ran downhill from second base to first.

Another Saints "comedy" involves Bob Newcomb, Anand Shah and Mike Snow. Long story short, Bob was injured in the closing moments of a basketball game when Anand hit him in the face with a point blank pass. Bob, all 6'6" of him, went down like a shot and had to be helped off the floor.

While I took Bob to a nearby hospital, the rest of the team stopped at a local restaurant on the way back to our hotel. Thankfully, Bob's x-rays proved negative. Arriving back at our hotel with nothing to do, he and I began to plot a way to get back at Anand, who was a rookie on his first crusade.

Our scheme was simple: Bob would lay motionless in his bed with a ketchup-soaked bandage wrapped around his head. When Anand returned from dinner, I was to invite him up to Bob's room, telling him that Bob's condition was grave. On the spur of the moment, I solicited some Saints veterans to help with the prank and they played their parts masterfully.

As Anand entered the dimly lit room, several of our players were hovering over Bob's listless body. Instinctively, Anand and his roommate Mike knelt by Bob's bed and started to pray. On cue, Bob moaned a few times and with each moan, Anand's prayers intensified. Finally, Bob "regained consciousness" and lurched toward Anand, seeking to extract his revenge. At that point, everyone broke into spontaneous laughter while Anand marveled at Bob's miraculous "healing".

A potentially serious injury occurred at the Delaware Correctional Center in Smyrna back in the mid 90's. Don Conner was playing left-center field when a long fly ball was hit to his right. Taking after the ball at top speed, Don failed to notice the 30-foot tall light pole in his way. In full stride, Don collided with the pole and for an agonizing moment, we didn't know the extent of his injuries. Miraculously, he only suffered a mild concussion and a small cut above his eye.

When our softball team returned to Smyrna the following season, all of the inmates wanted to meet Don. They were relieved to see that he was unharmed and to this day, many of them swear that the pole remains tilted from the collision.

Speaking of collisions (and concussions!), what makes a 160-pound second baseman think that he can run over a 220-pound catcher? I have asked myself that question many times since trying to score a run at the Otisville Correctional Institution in upstate New York. I guess my football instincts took over when I saw that I was going to be tagged out at home. And so, I lowered my shoulder and tried to bowl the catcher over, hoping to dislodge the ball.

Unfortunately, the only thing I dislodged was my consciousness as my teammates had to assist me to the bench where I remained for the duration of the game.

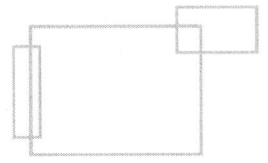

Four Score and Seven...
2007-2027

"Most assuredly, I say to you, he who believes in Me, the works that I do he will do also; and greater works than these he will do, because I go to My Father." John 14:12

History buffs will instantly recognize these four words – "Four score and seven" - as the beginning of Abraham Lincoln's memorable Gettysburg Address. Delivered in 1863, just 87 years after the start of the American Revolution, it reminded those in attendance of the sacrifices made by their forefathers as well as by those soldiers who had recently fallen on that sacred battlefield.

What a tragedy it would be for those sacrifices to have been offered in vain! Similarly, how tragic it would be if the sacrifices made and the lessons learned during the Saints first 20 years didn't result in a stronger, more far-reaching and even more Christ-honoring ministry. With this in mind, I want to lay out my personal vision for The Saints Prison Ministry for the next generation.

It's a simple mathematical equation. More teams mean more games in more prisons, which in turn means more inmates being exposed to the gospel message. With that in mind, it is my desire to see new Saints teams touring the Mid Atlantic States, saturating those institutions with the Good News of Jesus Christ.

Likewise, as we receive more and more invitations from prisons across the United States and in other countries, I see a need to establish additional regional branches. Our Western Branch in Colorado Springs should serve as a prototype for similar branches throughout the U.S. It simply makes sense, and would be much more ministry and cost-effective, to have local teams ministering in their own geographic areas instead of flying or busing teams from New Jersey all across the country.

With the advent of additional sports teams – and a corresponding increase in the demand for discipleship and aftercare - there will be a growing need for a national ministry headquarters. Missionary athletes will need a place to train and volunteers will need a place to grade Bible lessons. Our current facilities are nearly maxed out, and our staff and storage needs will only grow as our ministry expands.

I also envision the possibility of our headquarters complex having its own transitional housing. Ex-offenders enrolled in our affiliate, Lives in Transition, could reside there while they complete our six-month program. While there, they could also learn trades by caring for the complex itself, cooking for staff and landscaping the grounds. Additional housing could be built to accommodate visiting teams of missionary athletes who come to receive training in prison ministry.

Other ministry areas I would like to see the Saints address include a preventative outreach to at-risk youth in the inner-city, a ministry specifically to female prisoners, and an outreach to victims and their families. Prisoners' children, who are innocent victims of crime and also five times more likely to be incarcerated themselves, should be part of any comprehensive prison ministry. Finally, there is a growing need for criminal justice reform as sentencing guidelines become more and more antiquated.

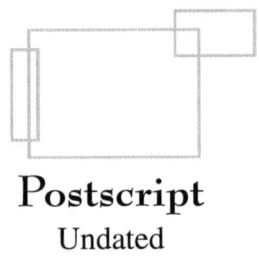

Postscript
Undated

"...being confident of this very thing, that He who has begun a good work in you will complete it until the day of Jesus Christ." Phil 1:6 (NKJV)

This is my life verse and it continues to minister to me on an almost daily basis, providing both comfort and inspiration. First, it reminds me that it was God who began a work in me and that - despite my shortcomings - it is indeed a "good" work. Additionally, it assures me that He will complete that same good work. And so, I can rest confidently in the fact that God knows exactly what He is doing and has the power to make good on His promises. In other words, the pressure is off me and on Him, and I kind of like it that way.

However, I must admit that at times, my life doesn't exactly resemble a "good work". To my shame, I have failed my Savior more times than I care to remember. Some of those failures have negatively affected my family and others have damaged the ministry to which God so graciously called me. Perhaps my most grievous sin is not always being as "willing" to heed God's voice as I was back in Williamsburg so many years ago.

After all these years, I remain very much a "work in progress." I guess I could say the same thing about The

Saints Prison Ministry. And yet, if there is one thing I have learned over the past 20 years it is simply this – that the key to personal fulfillment and true happiness is being in the center of God's will for your life. Yes, I know it sounds too elementary to be true, but I have also found that the key to discovering His will is simply being "willing." He will do the rest. This basic concept is equally applicable to a 47-year old man or a 20-year old ministry. Hopefully, the future is bright for both.

To paraphrase the Apostle Paul, "this one thing" I know…there is no shame in surrendering unconditionally to Jesus Christ. In fact, I am convinced that complete capitulation to the One who created me and then saved me is the greatest victory of all.

Our family's first prayer card in 1994.

Loading up the van for another softball crusade in the early 90's.

For several seasons in the mid-90's, we fielded two different basketball teams.

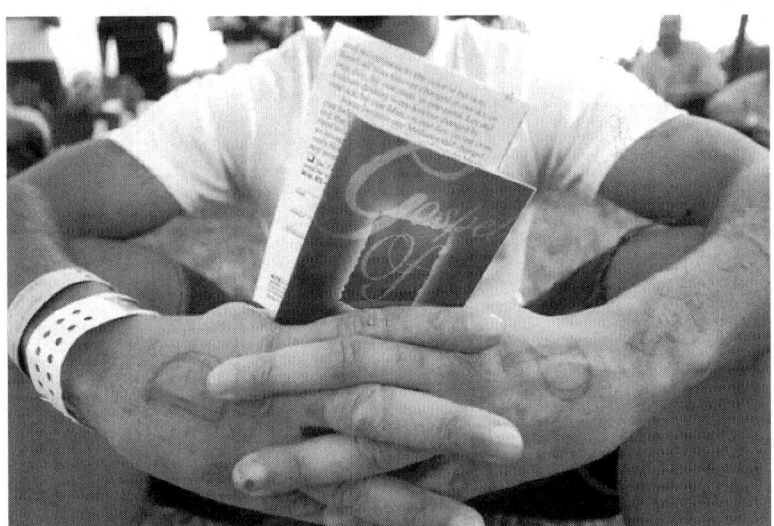

God promises that His Word will never return void.

Our first "Panhandle Crusade" in 1997.

Preparing to leave on a softball crusade, circa 1998.

Allegheny Mountain Crusade Team, August 1999.

Men for whom Christ died.

Our "Panhandle II Crusade" to Florida in 2002.

Visiting the Baseball Hall of Fame in Cooperstown, New York on our
Adirondack Mountain Crusade in 2002.

We formed a soccer team in 2003 in order to better reach Latino prisoners with the Gospel.

Two of our dedicated volunteers - Elaine Stephens (foreground), who has been with the ministry since it's inception, and Ruth McLaughlin (background), who continued to grade inmate Bible lessons well into her 90's.

Our softball teams have hosted several preseason tournaments to recruit new players.

Our Saints Basketball Team in Otisville, New York, circa 2004.

Atop the Space Needle in Seattle on our Pacific Northwest Crusade in 2005.

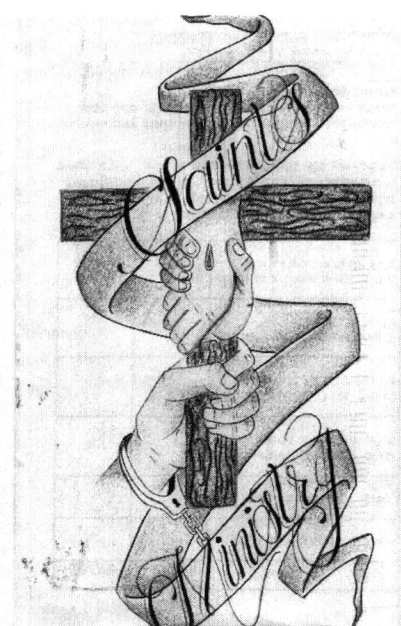

There are some very talented artists behind bars. Here's just one example.

Partnering with Gloucester County Community Church has helped us reach even more prisoners for Christ.

Other churches periodically minister under The Saints banner. Here are the Mount Vernon Baptist Saints from Richmond, Virginia.

Learning from the best. Tony Lawry coached our basketball team for more than 10 years.

Inmate morale soars when one of our teams comes to visit. Here Butch Smith and Ed Rentz share some laughs with a prisoner in Oneida, New York.

Frank Zeidler, Bud Collins, Steve Teisen and me enjoying some fellowship on one of our South Carolina crusades.

We occasionally scrimmage area Christian colleges to recruit future Missionary Athletes. Here Ed "Chief" Tarpey wins the tap while Don Conner and Kevin Harvey look on.

Playing as many as four games in one day can take a real toll.

Part of our "America's Southwest Crusade Team" that ministered in
New Mexico.

The same New Mexico Crusade Team following a muddy tripleheader.

Prisoners bowing in prayer on a recent crusade.

Steve Teisen leading a prisoner to Christ.

Rich Burns and Rob Fogel lead Arizona state inmates in prayer.

"Dr. John" Kolonich poses with an inmate brother in Christ.

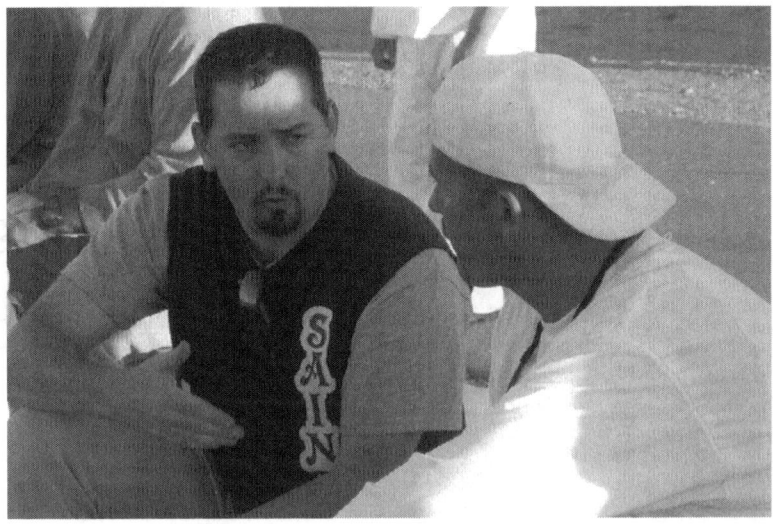

Rob Brown ministers to a prisoner one-on-one.

We continue to be burdened for inner-city youth. Here our basketball team "mixes it up" with teens at the Christy Recreation Center in West Philadelphia.

All of our games end with a prayer circle.

The Saints Prison Ministry has been using athletics to reach inmates with the Gospel of Jesus Christ since 1987. Our teams have collectively played in excess of 1,700 games behind prison walls in softball, basketball, volleyball, and soccer, resulting in over 15,000 professions of faith.

We regularly correspond with more than 25,000 men and women in over 400 prisons, from as near as South Jersey to as far away as South Africa. The Jericho Discipleship Program conducts in-prison Bible Studies in correctional facilities in New Jersey and also operates The Saints Bible Correspondence School. There are currently more than 2,500 inmates enrolled in the school, being discipled through Bible Study lessons and Pen-Pal letters.

Through our affiliate, Lives in Transition, and many ministry partners we are able to provide assistance to ex-offenders seeking a successful re-entry into society. Housing, clothing, basic toiletry essentials, and food supplies are just some of the forms of assistance available.

For more detailed information about The Saints Prison Ministry or to get involved, please visit our website at www.saintsprisonministry.org.

The Saints Prison Ministry
235 W. Main Street • P. O. Box 681 • Moorestown, NJ 08057
P: (856) 866-9428 • F: (856) 866-9727
www.saintsprisonministry.org